SMART BRAIN RIGHT BRAIN

An Introduction to Agricultural Engineering

Om KIDZ
An imprint of Om Books International

First Published in 2021 by

Om Kidz | Om Books International

Corporate & Editorial Office
A-12, Sector 64, Noida 201 301
Uttar Pradesh, India
Phone: +91 120 477 4100
Email: editorial@ombooks.com
Website: www.ombooksinternational.com

Sales Office
107, Ansari Road, Darya Ganj
New Delhi 110 002, India
Phone: +91 11 4000 9000
Email: sales@ombooks.com

Author: Shweta Sinha
Editor: Kirti Pathak
Art & Design: Anshuman Pandey, Gaurav Bhandari, Harish Arya

ISBN: 978-93-5276-845-5

Printed in India

10 9 8 7 6 5 4 3 2 1

CONTENTS

1. On the Farm

On the countryside, you can see farmland stretched all around you. A farm is a piece of land used to grow plants for food. Some farms raise animals, while some farms do both.

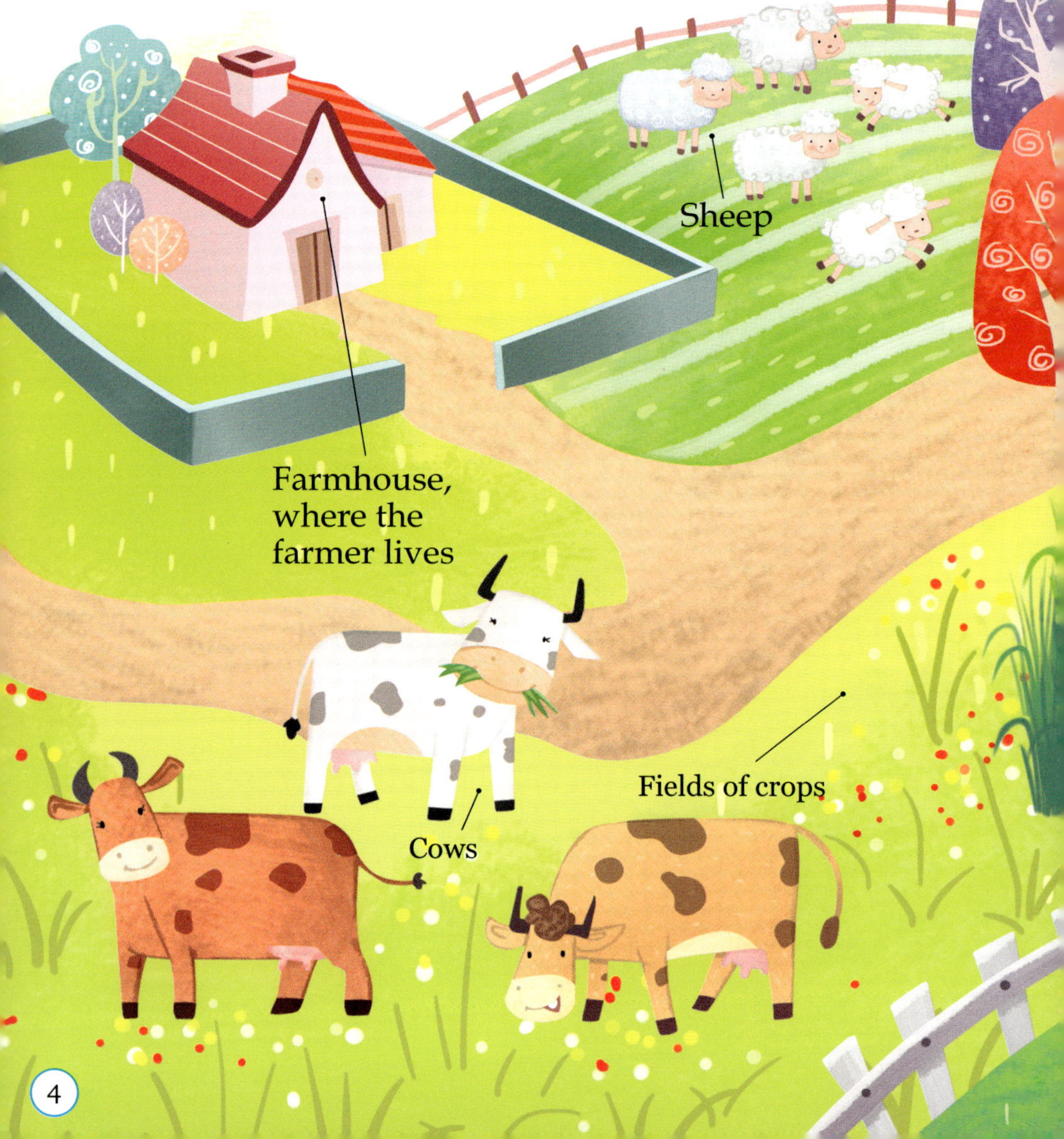

POCKET FACT

People who grow crops and raise animals on a farm are called farmers.

Agriculture and Engineering

Agriculture (say: agree-kul-chur) is another word for farming. Agriculture provides us the food we eat daily. It involves a lot of hard work and long hours on the farm.

Agricultural engineers are people who help farmers improve the crop production on their farms.

POCKET FACT

Crops are living plants grown by farmers. Crops can be grown for food, medicines, fibre for clothes or other materials like rubber and wood.

Agricultural engineers use science and technology to:

- Build machines and tools to use on a farm.
- Design and supervise the construction of farm buildings.
- Work on systems that provide power and water to farms.
- Help farmers produce more food by developing better seeds and keeping the soil healthy.

DID YOU KNOW?

Like us, even plants get affected by diseases. Genetic engineers are trying to modify plants to resist diseases.

2. Soil and Food Production

Different crops grow in different types of soil. Farmers choose the crops to grow depending on the soil type on their farms. Fertilisers are added to the soil from time to time to keep it healthy.

Sandy Soil – Have you been to the sea coast? The soil there has lots of sand. Not many plants grow in sandy soil.

Suitable Crops – Melon, coconut, maize, millets and barley.

Clayey Soil—Clayey soil gets sticky when mixed with water. It is rock-hard when dry. Even though rich in organic matter, clayey soil is not good for many crops.

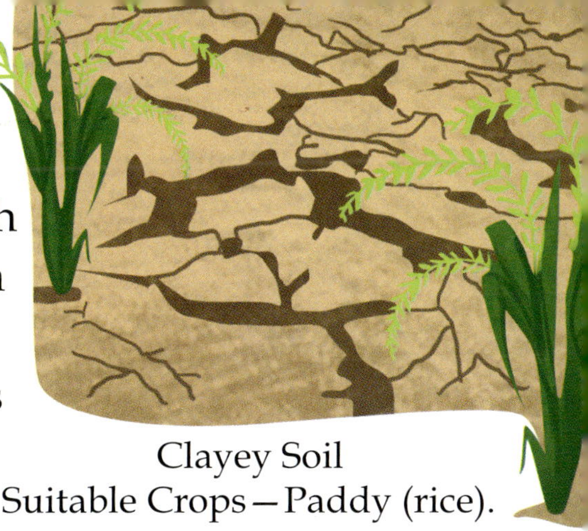

Clayey Soil
Suitable Crops—Paddy (rice).

Loamy Soil—This is the best kind of soil to grow plants. It can hold water and has nutrients. Nutrients and water help plants grow well.

Suitable Crops—Sugarcane, cotton, jute, pulses, oilseeds and vegetables.

POCKET FACT

Arable land is land that is used to grow crops for food.

3. Activity: Soil Shake Test

How can you find the soil type? Here is an easy test. You need:

- Jar with a lid.
- Pitcher of water.

1. Dig up some soil from the ground outside. Fill the jar half-way with it.

2. Add water to the jar until it is almost full. Close the lid and give the jar a nice shake. Now leave it overnight.

3. The soil-shake settles into layers.

How does your soil-shake look like?

- Clear water with sandy particles at the bottom – Sandy Soil.
- Water is cloudy with a thin layer of particles at the bottom – Clayey Soil.
- Fairly clear water with layered particles at the bottom – Loamy Soil.

4. Mighty Farm Machines

Growing crops and raising animals is a lot of hard work. A farmer takes the help of several machines for his work.

A **tractor** is a farmer's most trusted helper. It is a big, powerful vehicle with large wheels. It usually has only one seat for the driver.

A tractor can pull lots of heavy loads. The farmer uses the tractor to prepare the soil for planting and to harvest the crops.

DID YOU KNOW?

The treads on a tractor's tyres are bigger than your hand. The deep treads help grip the earth.

Digging up soil

The farmer attaches different machinery to the tractor for different jobs.

A **plough** has big teeth to turn the top soil over. It buries any plants or weeds that may be growing.

A **disc harrow** moves all the soil around. It chops off weeds and left-over crops.

A **cultivator** is used to till the land. It has sharp teeth which break up the soil. It prepares the land for planting seeds.

POCKET FACT

It is vital to prepare the soil well before planting seeds. Better soil gives better crops.

Planting seeds

Once the ground is tilled, it is ready for planting seeds. A **broadcast seeder** spreads seeds over a large area in one go. It is easy to use and is cheap.

This mighty machine is an **air seeder**. It shoots out seeds onto the ground. This seeder works best with small, round seeds. The air seeder is so huge that it has to be folded up when taking it down the road.

DID YOU KNOW?

People first started farming about 12,000 ago.

A **seed drill** sows seeds into the ground. It is more precise than the other seeders. It is good for cereal and other small seeds.

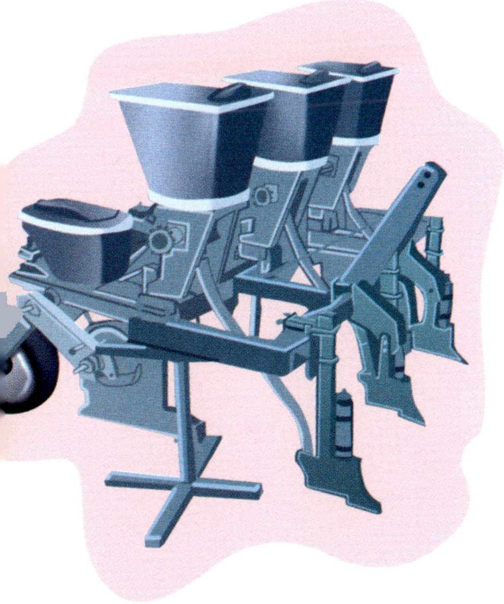

A **planter** sows seeds in rows on a field. A planter can handle large seeds like maize and beans.

POCKET FACT

Before there were farm machines, horses and oxen were used to do farm work.

More tractor tools

A **sprayer** or **sprinkler** sprays the field with liquid fertiliser. Fertiliser is a chemical that keeps crops healthy.

The **front loader** has long arms that let the farmer dig and move bulky things around. This is a very useful tool on a farm.

POCKET FACT

Tractors help farmers do their work with less number of workers.

Once the crops are ready, they need to be harvested.

A **harvester** cuts and collects these ripe plants. It then separates the grains from the stalks.

A **baler** makes rolls of stalks or grass.

DID YOU KNOW? The stalks of the ripe plants are used as hay bedding in the animals' pens.

Other farm equipment

A **tank truck** is used to carry water for plants and animals.

Animal droppings are mixed with straw to make manure. Manure keeps the soil healthy for crops.

A **manure spreader** spreads the manure all over the farm.

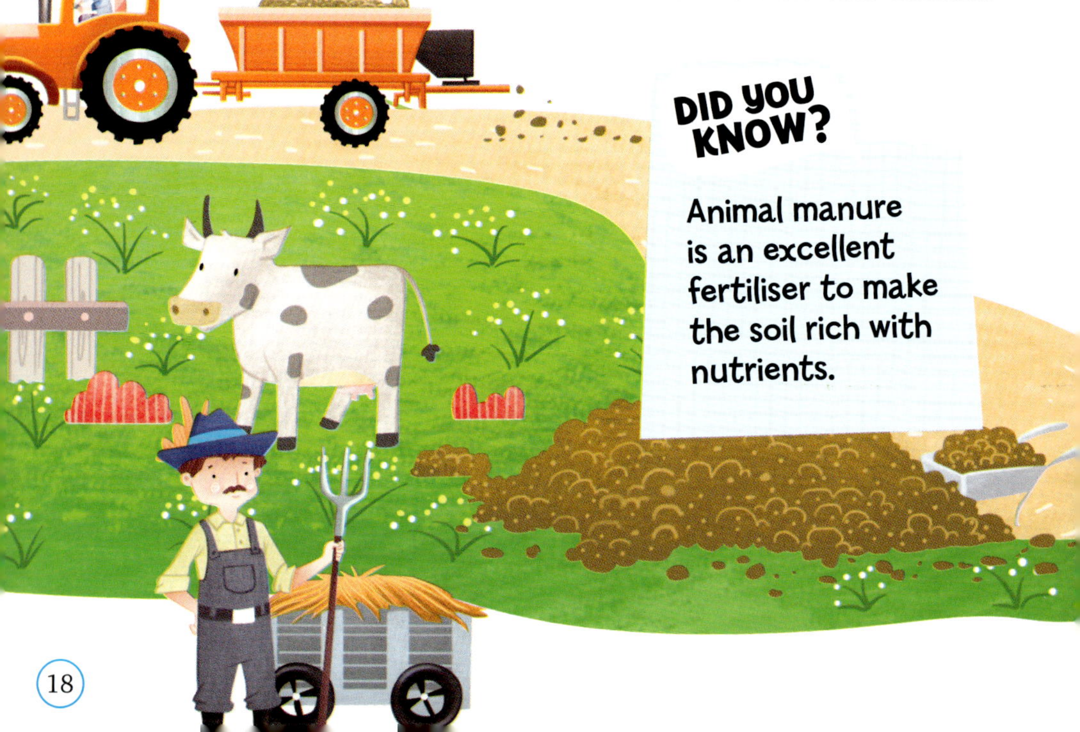

DID YOU KNOW?

Animal manure is an excellent fertiliser to make the soil rich with nutrients.

A **farm truck** is used to carry the farm produce to the market. It is also used to take a sick farm animal to the vet.

A **riding mower** is used to cut the grass and weeds growing on the farm.

A **mechanical tree shaker** is used to harvest the fruits from trees, especially pecan.

POCKET FACT

A farm that produces fruits or nuts is called an orchard, while one that produces grapes is called a vineyard.

Hand tools

Not all farm tools need a machine to power them. Here are some hand tools that farmers use.

A **pitchfork** is used to loosen the soil.

A **rake** is used for cleaning the ground

A **shovel** is used for removing trash, digging holes in the ground and moving soil.

DID YOU KNOW?

Some of the food that is widely eaten in your area was probably first grown by farmer in other far off countries.

A **wheelbarrow** is used to carry around trash, manure and also other equipment.

A **sickle** is a curved blade. It is used to harvest grain crops like rice.

An **axe** is a great tool to cut branches of trees and bushes.

POCKET FACT

Brazil is known as the 'sugar bowl' of the world. It produces more sugar than any other country.

5. Milk Production

1. Cows are milked every day using milking equipment. The milk is stored in refrigerated tanks.
2. The raw milk is transported in trucks to processing centres.
3. Milk is sterilised and pasteurised.
4. The processed milk is packaged. The packaged milk is transported to shops in trucks.
5. Customers buy the packaged milk in shops.

POCKET FACT

A life spent in raising animals on a farm is called a pastoral life.

6. Farming Eggs

The farmer keeps his hens in these huts. Hens lay eggs inside these huts.

The farmer collects the eggs soon after they are laid.

Eggs are transported by trucks to grading stations.

The eggs are washed and cleaned in a high speed tunnel washer. They are checked to remove any spoilt eggs.

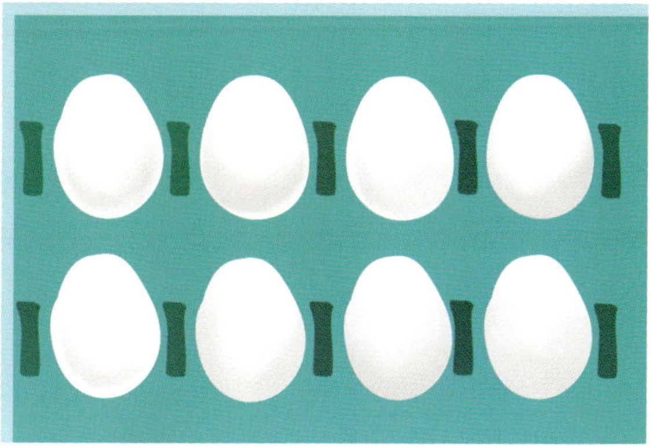

All okayed eggs are packaged in cartons. They are sent to the grocery store in refrigerated trucks.

POCKET FACT

Raising hens for their eggs is called poultry farming. Some farmers raise ducks and turkeys for eggs too.

7. Game: Let's Be a Farmer

- Your farm life begins
- 1
- Crack a great deal on a used tractor. Move ahead 2 spaces.
- 2
- 3
- 4
- Out of tractor fuel. Go back 1 space
- 5
- 6
- Land a local restaurant account. Move ahead 1 space
- 7
- 8
- Deer munch away half your plants. Go back 4 spaces.
- 9
- 10
- 11
- You made profit by selling eggs. Move ahead 3 spaces.
- 12
- Trade Places in the local farmer's market
- 13
- 14
- Hens run helter-skelter. You lose a couple of them. Go back 2 spaces.
- 15
- 16
- 17
- Neighbours complain of smelly pig poop. Lose a turn.
- 18
- First profitable year. Move ahead 2 spaces.
- 19
- End

Rules to Play:

- You need: A playing coin for each player and a dice.
- Roll the dice and move your coin the number of places on the dice.
- Lose a turn: the player loses a turn to play.
- Go forward/Go backward as the square says
- Trade Places: Swap places with an opponent.
- To finish, you must get the exact number to END. If you have more, count forward and backwards. For example if you are at 19, you need 1 on the dice. If you get 4, count 1 forward to END, then 3 backwards to 18.

Let's Get Active

Circle all these things you can find on a farm.

BARN	COWS	CROPS	DUCKS	FARMER	FARMHOUSE
FIELD	HENS	PIGS	SCARECROW	TRACTOR	VEGETABLES

S	C	A	R	E	C	R	O	W	I	A
H	V	J	C	R	O	P	S	B	B	S
F	Z	F	D	W	A	H	Z	A	Z	Q
A	H	E	N	S	P	T	O	R	R	M
R	I	S	P	O	I	P	N	N	L	S
M	G	G	J	A	G	D	U	C	K	S
H	U	C	O	W	S	G	L	O	G	A
O	K	Z	R	U	F	A	R	M	E	R
U	M	T	R	A	C	T	O	R	G	I
S	O	B	U	D	G	F	I	E	L	D
E	V	E	G	E	T	A	B	L	E	S

Farm tools

Jim has recently bought a new farm. He is confused about the tools and machines he needs. Can you help Jim match the right tool for the right job?

	Job	Tool
1.	Jim first needs to prepare the soil by tilling it.	Planter 
2.	Jim needs to lay down the seeds in a ploughed field.	Harvester 
3.	An agricultural engineer suggested Jim to spray fertiliser to get a better yield.	Plough 
4.	The wheat in Jim's farm is beginning to ripen. It is time to cut and harvest the grain.	Baler 
5.	Jim needs to make hay rolls for his sheep.	Sprayer/Sprinkler 

Milk Production

Can you help Jim figure out the correct order for Milk Production? The first job is numbered for you.

Milking

Packaging and transportation in refrigerated trucks

Transportation of raw milk

Feed the cows

1

Sale

Sterilisation

Colour me

Farmer McDonald's farm lost all its colours one morning. Can you help him put the colours back again?

GLOSSARY

Fuel	material such as coal, gas, or oil that is burned to produce heat or power
Grain	a small hard particle of a substance
Harvest	the process or period of gathering in crops
Nutrients	something that provides nourishment
Pasteurised	a process of partial sterilisation thus making the product safe for consumption
Precise	exact, accurate
Raw	not cooked
Refrigerated	used to keep or transport food or drink in a chilled condition
Ripe	developed to the point of readiness for harvesting and eating
Sow	plant seeds of a plant or crop
Stalk	the main stem of a plant
Sterilise	make something free from bacteria or other living microorganisms
Till	prepare and cultivate land for crops
Transport	take something from one place to another by means of a vehicle
Weed	a wild plant

ANSWERS

Page 28.

S	C	A	R	E	C	R	O	W	I	A
H	V	J	C	R	O	P	S	B	B	S
F	Z	F	D	W	A	H	Z	A	Z	Q
A	H	E	N	S	P	T	O	R	R	M
R	I	S	P	O	I	P	N	N	L	S
M	G	G	J	A	G	D	U	C	K	S
H	U	C	O	W	S	G	L	O	G	A
O	K	Z	R	U	F	A	R	M	E	R
U	M	T	R	A	C	T	O	R	G	I
S	O	B	U	D	G	F	I	E	L	D
E	V	E	G	E	T	A	B	L	E	S

Page 29. 1. plough 2.planter 3. sprayer/sprinkler
4. harvester 5. baler

Page 30. 1. Feed the cows 2. Milking
3. Transportation of raw milk
4. Sterilisation 5. Packaging and transportation in refrigerated trucks
6. Sale